School Places

by Soo Yee

T0052330

NATIONAL GEOGRAPHIC

Hampton-Brown

National Geographic and the Yellow Border are registered trademarks of the National Geographic Society.

National Geographic School Publishing
Hampton-Brown
www.NGSP.com

Printed in the USA.
Stromberg Allen, Tinley Park,IL

ISBN: 978-0-7362-7984-0

11 12 13 14 15 16 17 18 19 10 9 8 7 6 5

Acknowledgments and credits continue on the inside back cover.

This is a bus stop.

This is a classroom.

This is a lunch room.

LINE
B

This is a playground.

This is a school!